The
NIRODHA YOGA
of PATANJALI

The Transformation of Consciousness

REV. MICHAEL C. GADWAY

Contents

Introduction

There is an undercurrent of thought often found within Yoga communities that if we practice our asanas faithfully, pray hard enough, chant loud enough, and meditate deep enough, we do not have to face our karma. I have been told the mental restrictions we know as the kleshas do not have to be confronted but will melt in the fires of our devotions, or the chants of our mantras, if we just believe strong enough and hold on long enough. But this has not been my experience, nor is it validated in the ancient texts of India. To the contrary, these illuminated writings espouse the exact opposite; the entire symbolic Gita takes place on the battlefield of the mind and is about facing our psychological enemies in order to free ourselves from all mental restrictions to realize the truth within us. Patanjali states in his sutras that all karma has its roots in the kleshas and that karma will manifest when the time is ripe for expression. Nowhere does either of these great spiritual works deny the need to face what is ours. In fact, in *The Bhagavad Gita* when Arjuna drops his bow, symbolic of his karma, and states he will not fight, Krishna admonishes him for behavior unworthy of a spiritual warrior. Some karmas must be experienced, some must be overcome, and others may be transcended, but all karma must be confronted.

There is no scriptural evidence a God will descend from heaven and lift us out of the muck of our minds into a rarefied, clear state. If anything, the scriptures give us the means and inspiration to save ourselves. But before we can use any of the tools and techniques these sacred texts proffer, we must recognize and accept the psychological challenges we have created for ourselves through previous choices and behaviors.

No one is responsible for our current states of awareness and our ongoing circumstances but us, and no one is responsible for our freedom from these perceived restrictions but us. If we desire liberation and the freedom that comes with it, we must attend diligently to what is ours; a house will not clean itself, and to have a healthy garden, we must pull up the weeds by their roots.

All valid Yoga instruction presupposes one key element; the willingness of the Yogi to turn inward and bravely confront his or her own demons. Our demons are those mental restrictions and poisons of the psyche, as well as blurred states of awareness which prevent us from Self (Soul) Realization. They are like dams that block the river soul from flowing home to the ocean spirit. They are our own creations and only we can break them apart, dissolve them, and put an end to their obstructions.

The nirodha yoga of Patanjali comprises most of the first section titled 'Samadhi Pada' and may have made for a more accurate chapter title. Like most Sanskrit words, nirodha has several meanings; nirodha is defined as restraint or control, but also is used to indicate the action of restraining or controlling. Its root is $\sqrt{rudh}$, to restrict or to arrest. The nirodha yoga of Patanjali encompasses both the processes involved in restricting the citta and the vrtti, and the resulting effect of their restriction.

The ontological practices and procedures of nirodha yoga embraced in Patanjali's yoga and the yoga of Krishna found in the Bhagavad Gita include the pragmatic steps required to restrain, neutralize, and transform the citta and the vrtti. The sutras describe how to transmute the psyche into a clear instrument through which spirit may freely and fully express. These steps include meditation, prayer, and chanting as primary tools for Self-liberation, as well as the necessity of practicing the application of opposites and the yamas and the niyamas. Also highlighted in these sacred texts are friendliness, compassion, happiness, and equanimity as well as coming to a place of profound surrender and radical acceptance in order to purify the vessel through which the individualized Soul expresses.

It is a rare and intrepid individual who is willing to face themselves in the court of honest inner discrimination. I know how difficult and frightening the navigation of the interior psychological terrain can be. But we are Yogis, and we will do whatever it takes to be liberated.

As we move forward in our endeavor to be free, we must be clear why it is possible to emancipate ourselves from all mental restrictions and live-in spiritual freedom; we are individualized units of pure existence-being functioning through minds and bodies. We are made in the spiritual image of God. God is universal spirit; we are individuated spirit called souls. Our essence is God-stuff. There is nothing in our minds we cannot overcome because we are not what is in our minds. It is only our identification with these mental modifications that prevents us from recognizing this truth. There is no karma we cannot face down and be victorious over; in fact, we are here to overcome and transcend anything and everything which prevents us from experiencing the truth of our sacred existence. If it was not possible to be free, there would not be the spiritual science we know as Yoga teaching us how to do so.

It is our inexorable destiny to realize truth, awaken to our divinity, and to be forever free. To accomplish this, we must take responsibility for, and accept where we are now and the futures we have yet to create. Though we are not to blame for our current circumstances, we are responsible for them. To change our experiences in the world, we must change our consciousnesses. We must shift from our old mundane ways of viewing and interacting with the world and rise up to a higher, more spiritual way. It is not enough to think differently; we must be different. We must be authentic: existing, expressing, and delighting in the truth of our own being. We have unlimited potential waiting within us to express brilliantly unhindered by doubt, shame, and fear. We have only to take the first step in Yoga to begin the journey to Self-Realization and the freedom that awaits us all.

CHAPTER 1:

Yoga

I am the bubble, make me the sea.
— Paramahansa Yogananda

The term Yoga has become synonymous in the West with the beautiful and flowing physical practices we see in Yoga studios, gyms and on television, but there is much more to yoga than poses and postures.

Yoga is one of the six philosophical schools of thought or traditions in India known as the Astikas. We know it has been practiced in various forms in India for millennia, but its origins have been lost to antiquity; we lose its historical thread prior to its mention in the Rig-Veda, the oldest known spiritual text in the world, dated to circa 1500 BCE. The most plausible reason for this is before its mention in the Rig Veda, Yoga was an oral tradition passed down from teacher to student. This custom is part of a larger tradition known as Shruti, meaning 'that which is heard.' It is said the great seers of past ages heard the sacred science of Yoga during profound and mystical meditations and began to share it with others who were looking to liberate themselves from the delusions of the material world. Many scholars assert Yoga was the practical extension of Samkhya philosophy and has its roots in the subtle astral and causal realms. Students were once immersed in the philosophy of Samkhya before going on to practice Yoga. Philosophy and science were once blended and seen as interdependent, but over the centuries, the philosophical schools of Samkhya melted into obscurity while yoga continued to thrive in ashrams throughout India.

In the past, spiritual sanctions allowed only a Guru (spiritual teacher), who was ordained by his own Guru to represent the teachings, to orally share the liberating techniques of Yoga which limited its spread, keeping it an esoteric practice. With the modern era, Yoga became more accessible and began to be taught worldwide. But with that dissemination also came a watering down of the sacred science and its spiritual benefits were overshadowed by the physical advantages it created; the deep and mystical aspects of Yoga were subsumed into pop culture, and with the oversharing of information came a loss of inviolability. But there were a few bright flames that kept this profound and transformational discipline alive in the West including Paramahansa Yogananda and his direct disciple, my own Guru, Roy Eugene Davis. As authentic representatives of an unbroken lineage of Kriya Yoga Gurus, they kept the spiritual science of Yoga intact and unadulterated. Through them, it remained purely aligned with the ancient tradition of Yoga.

We must be careful not to imply that Yoga is a religion; it is not a religion. Yoga is an evidence based spiritual science available and applicable to all people regardless of religion, race, creed, color or gender. It is for those who want to escape the suffering of creation, emancipate themselves from the shackles of unknowing, and awaken to their true essence of being; it is the science of libera-tion. By codifying Yoga in Patanjali's Yoga Sutras, most scholars agree Yoga as a mystical art was transmuted into a philosophy. It can be further argued Yoga was in fact transformed by Patanjali's Yoga Sutras into a practicum and by doing so, made available to everyman.

The term Yoga in Patanjali's Yoga Sutras is used contextually in two ways; nowhere is Yoga defined in the Yoga Sutras. It is assumed the student has had the necessary preliminary training to know its various definitions and its intended uses. But this is not always the case; contemporary use of the word Yoga has evolved to have three distinctly different meanings.

In the West, when we say Yoga, most of us think of Hatha Yoga, the flowing series of poses known as asanas. Hatha Yoga means 'Union through forced-flow'. It was originally intended to prepare the body and mind through specific postures and breathing techniques for deeper states of meditation. Its practice unblocks energy, strengthens body and mind, balances physical and mental forces, and improves both physical and mental flexibility. With its practice, we learn to use both hemispheres of the brain more equally, allowing for higher cognitive func-tion and therefore more advanced states of perception.

Hatha was a natural extension of the pouring forth of prana through the body and mind in an act of self-maintenance and balance in preparation for more profound states of awareness. It was never intended to be practiced in isolation for its physical benefits alone. That came with the integration of

Yoga into modern culture.

In the Kriya Yoga tradition, Hatha Yoga is practiced in a more meditative state. We remain focused and calm allowing the prana the opportunity to flow unchecked through deep channels to heal, balance and uplift body, mind, and awareness. We gently flow into each asana with focus and calm, and by doing so train both the body and mind to remain intent on one point. This also assists the spiritual aspirant in better concentration and a clearer, more one-pointed focus during their meditation practice.

It may surprise some to know there is no mention of Hatha Yoga in Patanjali's Yoga Sutras. The only time the Yoga Sutras refer to an asana practice is in the section known as Ashtanga Yoga. There, it says only one's meditative asana should be fixed or firm, and comfortable. Nevertheless, a Hatha Yoga practice has become an integral part of the Yoga journey and should be practiced regularly for physical, mental, and spiritual benefits.

In Sir Monier-Williams Sanskrit-English dictionary we find over five dozen different and distinct definitions of the word Yoga. The Sanskrit root of the word Yoga is $\sqrt{yuj}$, which means 'to yoke,' implying the practice of Yoga joins and binds us to God, first in the specialized form of the Atman, then as the boundaries of ego dissolve, the universal formlessness of Brahma. The Yoga of Patanjali is, in this sense, the process of transforming the individual consciousness into a fit receptacle for the perfected demonstration of spirit; it is the science of spiritual Self-awakening.

The spiritual science of Yoga is enumerated and set forth within the Yoga sutras as a methodical and orderly body of knowledge presented in a sequential aphoristic format. Each sutra is a concise directive designed to guide the spiritual aspirant towards awakening. The clearing away of psychological debris that litters the mind, the cleansing of subtle soul sheaths, and the release of blocked energy patterns which prevent unrestricted Soul expression are required preparations leading to the primary goal of Yoga, enlightenment.

The process of Yoga, as found in Patanjali's Yoga Sutras, empowers the seeker to become Self-reliant with essential awakening tools that, when applied with dedication banish avidya, ignorance of our divine truth. By concurrently practicing profound meditation, as taught within the scriptures of Yoga, and putting into practice the clear how to live and think principles, also described within the text, the student cleanses and perfects the Soul vessels, inevitably evolving to clearer and higher states of awareness. Through the scientific method of Yoga, as outlined in Patanjali's Yoga Sutras, the individual progresses from a small confined and limited sense of self (ego) to the realization of Self as universal Spirit.

With the committed practice of Yoga, the restrictive borders of ego awareness are gradually expanded and with this expansion comes the dissolution of a separate sense of self. The obscuring veil of unknowing (Maya) becomes more transparent until one day it dissolves altogether, and any false sense of a separate self is once and for all banished as the soul awakens to its truth of universal oneness.

As well as being the term used in the sutras for the process of consciousness transformation, Patanjali also uses the word Yoga to mean 'union.' Patanjali writes in the second sutra of the first pada (quarter) that Yoga (union) is achieved by the restriction of the citta and the vrtti. The succeeding sutra states, "then the seer abides in its own form (Soul)". This is unambiguously Self-realization, a known-by-knowing experience.

Most scholars propose the union brought on by the restriction of the citta and vrtti (nirodha yoga) is with Isvara, but nowhere within the first pada is this assumption stated by Patanjali. It is not until nearly halfway through the first pada that dedication to Isvara is mentioned as a means to experience samadhi, also stating that samadhi is a precursor to direct insight.

It is often assumed that Yoga (union) is a synonym for samadhi, but a case can be made there is a subtle difference between the two. After all, not every samadhi experience is one of Self or God realization. This may also explain why the Yoga Sutras later differentiate between samadhi and samyama (perfect concentration). Some authors have argued the nirodha is a precursor to samadhi; a purified stage which leads to a higher experience. But it is clear in the sutras that when nirodha is experienced, the result is Self-realization. Nirodha is a direct means to liberation, not a staging ground for the next result.

Isvara is described in the first pada of the Yoga Sutras as that 'special purusa.' Many define purusa as self, but it has several meanings and is also known to be the "universal principle". The term Isvara has numerous definitions including the unspecialized field of spirit we call God. Isvara has evolved and changed over the centuries and it is unlikely at the time the sutras were composed, the author was implying the soul (Self) mentioned in the third sutra was synonymous with Isvara.

The ability to experience Yoga (union) by restricting the citta and the vrtti, and bringing them to a standstill, implies meditation is not the only means to achieve liberation. In fact, there is no mention of the need to meditate in order to experience this state in the first pada; this does not occur until the second pada. This implies meditation is only one tool of many available to us to realize union with the divine. There are saints in all traditions who reported having experienced superconsciousness and union with God, not having practiced formal meditation procedures. This is not to downplay the importance of meditation or its vital role in liberation, but to emphasize meditation is a vehicle and not the goal. The point here is to stress the significance of a more comprehensive spiritual approach. Yoga philosophy, which advocates Self-reliance and Self-responsibility in a more spiritually inclusive lifestyle, gives us numerous methods to transform the consciousness, all leading the devotee towards the goal of spiritual freedom. Taken together with meditation, they are powerful tools for the transformation of consciousness leading to the final result of liberation.

The first pada is dedicated to understanding the modifications of the mind and gives us a multitude of ways, including meditation, to first restrict and then remove them from influence. Patanjali gives the spiritual aspirant a collection of approaches to cleanse, overwrite, and dissolve the citta and the vrtti. Perhaps the ancient seers understood not every disciple of God has the same temperament or can use the same approach day in and day out, and therefore needs a variety of procedures in order to be successful. Yoga is not just for the hermit cave dweller who can dedicate eighteen hours a day to meditation, but is an effective approach for those householders with secular responsibilities as well.

All the procedures listed in the sutras, including meditation, can and should be applied collectively with a steadfast dedication in order to realize the goal of God union. To effectively transform individualized consciousness necessitates an integrated approach with a wholehearted and single-pointed commitment.

CHAPTER 2:

The Transformation of Consciousness

Calmness, gentleness, silence, self-restraint, and purity:
these are the disciplines of the mind.
— Bhagavad Gita

Yoga is far more than an armchair philosophy. It is parinama citta: the transformation of consciousness. To practice Yoga is to intentionally engage in the process of self-transformation in order to systematically dissolve the ego and thin the veil of Maya. This process leads us ever closer to the realization of our unity with the divine.

In order to participate and have experiences in the cosmic play, souls take on causal, astral, and physical sheaths. This putting on of soul vessels creates a false sense of distance between the soul and spirit. There is a veiling of reality and the soul becomes identified with the various sheaths and their inherent complexities. With this donning of soul layers comes a forgetting of the Self and the soul's knowing of its existence-being is clouded. Seers tell us ignorance of our true nature is the primary cause of our suffering. Yoga gives the devotee a practical stratagem for experiencing the Self, thereby effectively removing suffering. The primary goal of Yoga is to eliminate avidya and establish wisdom-based discrimination, viveka; we are then able to discern between the real and unreal. An awakening to our authentic nature occurs when all that encompasses the soul is purified and brought to utter stillness. The distortion of perception caused by the motion of the mind and soul vessels is clarified by the experience of alert, absolute tranquility. Truth is not perceived but experienced; the light of the soul shines forth in the purified mind. Then a dawning of realization occurs within the field of awareness; the spiritual aspirant has an instantaneous realization of 'I am that.'

The nirodha yoga of Patanjali's first pada clearly enumerates what we are transforming and restraining; there are two distinct categories listed in the first pada that must be transformed, purified, and brought to a standstill, to allow Soul-realization to blossom in the individual's field of awareness.

The first of these is citta; this term is not described within the sutras and therefore has invited endless argument about its exact definition. The root of citta is $\sqrt{cit}$, which means 'to perceive'. Most Sanskrit experts interpret this as consciousness, and some have defined it as 'mind stuff'. A few, including my own Guru, have proposed citta is an inclusive field of awareness. Paramahansa Yogananda stated the term citta includes manas, buddhi, prana, and ahamkara. Regardless of how we choose to interpret citta, we should recognize it is, as Vyasa pointed out, one thing. Though it may have various aspects, they are inextricably entwined and must be understood and approached as a whole unit. No oversimplification of the word operates within the necessary parameters to encompass its entire meaning. To refer to citta as a multidimensional field of awareness including manas, buddhi, prana, and ahamkara is, for our purposes, the most accurate description. To better understand citta, the following paragraphs will define and analyze each part of it.

The Sanskrit term manas means 'of the mind'. The root of manas is $\sqrt{man}$, defined as 'to think'. Manas is best interpreted as 'the thinking principle'. Manas is a field used by the soul to process and store information pertaining to the sensory world. Our minds are individual units of universal mind. Our brains are organs of our minds and have corresponding versions in each of the soul vessels. It is the individual mind that is taken with and used by the soul from lifetime to lifetime.

Buddhi has no direct English equivalent. Buddhi is intuitive and discriminating intelligence. It is one of the tattvas (aspect of reality) identified in the Samkhya philosophical system. It is here where discrimination blossoms and where the light of the soul is reflected when Self-realization dawns.

Prana is one of the three cosmic forces making up the multiverse. It is the subtlest form of energy; all other energies in the physical realm are derived from prana. Paramahansa Yogananda described it, in his commentary on the Bhagavad Gita, as "intelligent energy". Prana is quantumly entangled and circulates throughout the body/brain soul vessel to animate, enliven, and transmit cellular intelligence. Two of the accepted definitions of Prana are 'constant motion' and 'primal breath'.

Ahamkara is literally translated as 'I am-ness.' It is that false separate sense of self the soul acquires when taking on the various sheaths in the process of incarnating. In the West, we refer to this as ego. This should not be confused with egotistical, an inflated sense of self.

The next category to be transformed, according to Patanjali, is vrtti. The root of this word is $\sqrt{vrt}$, meaning to whirl or to revolve. The most common interpretations are mind fluctuations or mental modifications. Again, Patanjali does not define the word. The vrtti are ways the soul, through the mind, views the world, takes in and processes information. They are perceptions of the mind and often occur as patterns played out repeatedly for individuals. We may better understand vrtti as states of awareness with defined boundaries. The word implies the soul stands at the center of a whirlwind of alternating thought patterns and viewpoints. Identified with these patterns, unable to remain neutral observers, people experience joy when the vrtti are perceived as pleasant and suffer when they are perceived as painful. It is the vrtti philosophers are referring to when saying ordinary consciousness is blurred with movement or misperceptions.

According to Patanjali there are five types of vrtti, and each type may be afflicted or not afflicted. These five vrtti are: valid acquiring of information (cognition), invalid acquiring of information (error), imagination, memory, and sleep. These states are described fully within the sutras themselves.

It is important to know within the Yoga Sutras there are two other categories that need purification and transformation: the kleshas and the samskaras. Both these categories are conditions of manas, the mind. The kleshas are not delineated within the first pada as part of nirodha yoga and the samskara receive only a cursory mention in the eighteenth sutra. This disjuncture is one of the many reasons listed by scholars suggesting there were multiple authors of Patanjali's Yoga Sutras.

Though the word klesha is used in the first pada, it is not differentiated as a category of awareness until the second pada. The Sanskrit root of kleshas is $\sqrt{klist}$, meaning 'to afflict' or 'to trouble'. The kleshas are afflictions or poisonings of the mind. They can be described as clouds that block the sun. While the kleshas dominate the mind, the light of the soul is obstructed from shining clearly in the mind. We are unable to 'see' the truth of our being and we are prevented from the realization of 'I am that'. The kleshas are fivefold and include, avidya (ignorance), asmita (ego), raga (attachment), dvesa (aversion), and abhinivesah (clinging to life and its processes).

Also found in Patanjali's Yoga Sutras is the term samskara. As with much of the terminology within the sutras, Patanjali does not define or describe this word. Samskara is derived from two-word roots: $\sqrt{sam}$, meaning 'to put together,' and $\sqrt{kr}$, 'to do'; the word karma has the same root. The samskaras are the mental impressions left in the mind from thoughts, feelings, intentions, and actions. Paramahansa Yogananda described them to be like grooves in a record. These grooves in the mind reveal themselves as psychological patterns and emotional responses that are often generated from the subconscious.

Taken together, the citta, vrtti, kleshas, and samskara are the components of our karmic package. These are the contents, conditionings, and restrictions of the mind that have been accumulated and stored over lifetimes and must be confronted, neutralized, dissolved, and finally transcended.

CHAPTER 3:

A Brief Overview of Nirodha Yoga

First, have a definite, clear practical ideal; a goal, an objective.
— Aristotle

The first pada of Patanjali's Yoga Sutras titled *Samadhi-Pada* contains 51 sutras and is written in an almost diagrammatical form. It serves as both an outline for an inclusive and integrated yoga practice as well as a step-by-step how to guide.

The first and second sutras are introductory sutras that familiarize the reader with Yoga and describe its process. It then goes on in the third and fourth sutras to discuss Self-realization and the Self in relationship to existence-being.

Sutras five through eleven enumerate and describe the vrtti (mental fluctuations) and their influences. From sutra twelve to sutra sixteen, Patanjali tells us how to restrict the vrtti through practice and dispassion.

Sutras seventeen through twenty describe the result of Yoga as having two levels of direct insight into truth, then describe the results of these experiences and what precedes them.

The next two sutras, twenty-one and twenty-two, examine the levels of commitment needed by the Yogi for success. These are followed by sutras twenty-three through twenty-eight, characterizing Isvara as the supreme Self, aloof and untouched by nature, and approachable through devotion.

Sutras twenty-nine through thirty-two list the obstacles a Yogi must face and how to overcome them. These are followed by sutras thirty-three through thirty-nine giving specific means to restrict and neutralize the vrtti and sutra.

The fortieth sutra simply states the clarification of the mind results in mastery of the mind from its smallest component to its greatest.

Sutras forty-one through forty-five describe the four stages of samadhi, leading to the final stage of experiencing pure existence being without support of form.

The remaining sutras, forty-six through fifty-one, describe first samadhi with 'seed,' then samadhi without 'seed'.

CHAPTER 4:

The Sutras of Nirodha Yoga

This is not the path of escapism you know.
— Paramahansa Yogananda
to Roy Eugene Davis

PADA I, SUTRA 1

Atha-yoga-anusasanam

Now-yoga-instruction

Now that a preliminary study in Samkhya philosophy has occurred, including the manifestation, cause, and unfoldment of creation, and the soul's freedom from bondage and suffering, the practice of Yoga and its techniques can begin.

What came before, until the common era, was an intense and prolonged study of Samkhya philosophy. Most scholars now refer to the entirety of the system as Samkhya-Yoga. But, the program of study with preparation by philosophy first, followed by practice second, faded into obscurity long ago. They have blended into a single tradition which has created many false assumptions about Yoga's purpose and practice. Because of the lack of understanding caused by little to no philosophical training, a romanticizing of Yoga has occurred leading to unrealistic expectations and an increase in fantasy-based spirituality.

But if we were to study Samkhya philosophy by itself, the knowledge gained would not lead to liberation; liberation from suffering and delusion cannot be obtained by knowledge alone. It requires realization. To practice a discipline well, we must first understand the philosophy behind it and the purpose of it, but to learn a philosophy without a practicum produces inept pseudointellectuals.

Yoga is not a cure-all or a path of escapism. It is a course in radical acceptance and scientific training design to systematically dissolve the ego. Yoga, once part of a hidden mysticism and the practical extension of Samkhya, has become a technique-based philosophy unto itself.

Samkhya and Yoga are integrated parts of the same whole and one should not be practiced without the other.

Pada I, Sutra 2

Yoga-citta-vrtti-nirodha

Yoga-multidimensional field of awareness (manas, buddhi, asmita, prana)-mental modifications-process of restraining and the restraint of

The process of Yoga is the practice of restraining the citta and the vrtti and Yoga (union) occurs when the citta and vrtti are restrained.

The second sutra describes how union with the Self is achieved. This is the most misquoted sutra of Patanjali's Yoga Sutras and the least understood. The second sutra is not a definition of Yoga as many commentators would have you believe. It is a description of how Yoga is achieved and its results.

Yoga (union) occurs when the citta and vrtti are rendered motionless. When they are restrained and can no longer blur a perception of the Self shining within the buddhi of the mind, the result is a union of the Yogi's consciousness with that which it is: the soul.

Yoga is also the ontological and soteriological processes and procedures involved in achieving this result.

Pada I, Sutra 3

Tada drastuh sva-rupe vasthanam

Then seer own-form abiding

Established in Yoga (Union) the soul no longer identifies with the modification of consciousness (citta and vrtti) and remains Self-realized.

It is here in the third sutra Patanjali gives us the definition of Self-Realization. When the soul (seer) no longer identifies with the undulating waves of consciousness and is instead fully aware of its true nature, ignorance (avidya) has been banished and the Self (Soul) now permanently dwells in realization of its own existence-being.

PADA I, SUTRA 4

Vrtti-sarupyam-itaratra

Fluctuation-with the form of (conforms to)-otherwise

When not established in the existence-being of Self-realization, the soul identifies with the fluctuations of the mind.

When we are not anchored in the infinite, the soul identifies with the citta, vrtti, samskara, and kleshas of the mind. We associate the psycho-mental waves of thoughts, feelings, habits, and mental patterns and the truth of our being as one and the same. There is a temporary forgetting of our spiritual truth. We forget we are souls functioning through bodies and minds, but we are neither the body nor the mind and its contents.

Intrinsic to the Yoga process is the practice of learning to remain the observer. This practice requires patience and equanimity. We must learn to step back and become aware of ourselves as that which stands behind the mind watching: the seer/soul.

PADA I, SUTRA 5

Vrttayah pancatayah klista-aklistah

Fluctuations fivefold afflicted-non afflicted

The fluctuations of the mind are fivefold and may be perceived as distressful or not distressful.

According to the Yoga Sutras, the mind perceives, takes in, and processes information in five distinct ways; there are five fields of awareness common to all human minds. These perceptions can be seen by the observer as causing suffering or not.

The fluctuations themselves do not cause distress; it is the perceiver's processing and interpretation of the information in relationship to the kleshas with the gunas influences which may or may not cause them to be perceived as distressful.

Pada I, Sutra 6

Pramana-viparyaya-vikalpa-nidra-smrtayah

*Valid cognition-misapprehension (error)-
conceptualization (forming a concept or idea) -sleep-memory*

The five fluctuations of the mind are: valid knowledge and understanding-mistaken belief or mistaken interpretation (error)-imagination-sleep-memory.

Most people do not seek out information; they seek out validation. The mind is often shaded with bias and molded by subconscious habits, drives, tendencies, and behaviors. Even the acquisition of valid information does not guarantee sound reasoning. Part of the spiritual maturation process is developing and nurturing our discrimination (viveka), while remaining inwardly in tune and connected with our enlightenment tradition and its teachers. Learning to use information in real-world application from an altruistic frame of reference while remaining unattached to results, is perhaps the best way to move through the world.

Two or more of these five states of awareness are often operating concurrently. They may be blended and are often shaded by the influence of our past experiences, current understanding, perceptions, attachments, aversions, and the gunas. While we may mentally process part of the information taken in correctly, it is possible to be in error with another part of the information bundle.

To detach from this egocentric viewpoint, yoga teaches us to learn to inwardly remain the observer. We take a step back from our mental processes and watch with curiosity as experiences and perceptions unfold and change. We detach from a judgmental attitude to one of open curiosity that employs the use of reason and intuition in the discriminative process.

Pada I, Sutra 7

Pratyaksa-anumana-agamah pramanani

Perception-inference-testimony valid cognition

Valid knowledge and understanding may come from direct perception, inference, and the testimony of qualified sources.

Valid information may be acquired directly through the senses; we can see, hear, and become aware of something either actively or passively. We can also know simply by knowing, an ability of the soul when we are mentally clear and calm.

We may also infer information; we can deduce or conclude from the evidence and reasoning before us.

And finally, we can take, on faith, the information provided for us by the educated testimony of enlightened teachers transmitted either orally or by the written word.

However, acquiring valid information does not mean the information will be processed correctly. For this, we must learn to develop and rely on the buddhi; the ability to recognize and know truth intuitively.

Pada I, Sutra 8

Viparyayo mithya-jnanam-atad-rupa-pratistham

Misapprehension-erroneous-knowledge-not that-form-foundation

Misapprehension (error) is false knowledge, founded on misjudging something or someone based on appearance and form.

Appearances can be deceiving. How something appears may or may not represent its true form or intent. We must look behind appearances and presentation to see the spiritual truth of every living creature.

If we remain calm and centered, with our attention placed at the sixth chakra, the part of the mind (manas) we refer to as the buddhi, will intuit the truth of what is placed before us. We can know and understand the truth of someone or something simply by intending to know. This comes with practice or as a result of spiritual awakening and is a faculty of buddhi, direct perception.

Pada I, Sutra 9

Sabda-jnana-anupati vastu-sunyo vikalpah

Words-knowledge-following (result of) object-empty conceptualization

Conceptualization (forming a concept or idea) is a result of verbal knowledge without an object.

Abstract idealization and imagination are functions and products of the human mind. It is possible to use the mind to create entire mental landscapes and situations even when the senses are not providing information.

This function of the mind has positive and negative polarities; it can be used to assist us in problem solving, possibility thinking, and inspirational imagination. We can use it to imagine solutions to difficult circumstances, and ways to move forward through life, deriving new, previously unthought of resolutions to seemingly unsolvable problems. However, we can also use it to dissociate from reality, hiding within the recesses of our imaginations as a way of escapism.

It is possible to consciously use this faculty of the mind constructively; we can use it to create meaning for ourselves as an operative tool of choice. We can choose to see conditions as fortuitous opportunities for growth potential or adversities which must be either overcome or succumbed to.

It is the ability of the mind to form unsupported concepts and ideas that allows us to expand the limits of the mind, exploring horizons beyond our current boundaries of paradigm and concept. In doing so, we can break free from our mental constraints and our limited sense of awareness, loosening restricting mental conditions with imagination and conceptualization.

Pada I, Sutra 10

Abhava-pratyaya-alambana vrttir-nidra

Not becoming-intention-founded on fluctuations-sleep

Sleep is founded on the intention of non-becoming.
Sleep holds no intent to become, only the renewing experience of existence-being.

Whether we are conscious of it or not, spiritual awakening is continual and ongoing. And although the soul does not need to rest, the mind and body must have time to recover from the challenges inherent in the spiritual growth process.

We are participating in a progression of spiritual becoming. To awaken in truth, the mind and body must evolve into more fit instruments of spiritual expression, and this often challenges established mental and physical habits, routines, and behaviors.

Sleep is a temporary reprieve from the trial and tribulations of becoming by resting in a restorative state of unconscious existence-being while the mind and body reorganize, heal, and recharge.

PADA I, SUTRA 11

Anubhuta-visaya-asmpramosah smrtih

Experienced-condition-recollection memory

Memory is recalling a previously experienced condition.

The human memory does not necessarily recall much of what is experienced, but what it does remember is surprisingly accurate. What this tells us is most memory is selective; we remember what interests us or holds our attention, whether in a positive or negative way. It also indicates we can retain an accurate account of what we experience when we apply our attention and focus. What is important to us in this life can be retained and the lessons we learn can be applied to new and unfolding experiences.

When the mind (manas) has imprinted these lessons, it carries them forward as samskara, some positive and some negative, into the future. These samskara, patterns of thought, can be used to make life enhancing choices or stay away from experiences which are life diminishing.

Memory is a function of the mind and it is the mind the soul takes with it from lifetime to lifetime. In this way, we do not have to learn the same lessons over and over. We can recall information, whether it is conscious or subconscious recall, and apply it towards bettering the present. There is no need to repeatedly experience the same karmas. We can simply apply what we have learned and remembered, in order to choose wisely. In this way, we are not fated to experience the same challenges again and again.

PADA I, SUTRA 12

Abhyasa-vairagyabhyam tan nirodhah

Practice–dispassion that restriction

Restraint of the citta and the vrtti occur as a result of practice and dispassion.

The practice of Yoga encompasses the processes and procedures involved in purifying, transforming, and bringing to a standstill the citta and the vrtti. We train ourselves to actively cooperate in the unfolding process of self-transformation, preparing our bodies and minds to be luminous vessels through which spirit flows.

Learning to still all the moving parts involved in the human condition while remaining ever watchful as the observer/seer, requires an ongoing surrendered focus and a humble determination. We must practice, without attachment to results, the life-changing techniques which bring about the transmutation of spirit expressing, without restriction through the body and mind.

PADA I, SUTRA 13

Tatra-sthitau-yatno bhyasah

There-remaining in that state-effort practice

The effort of remaining in that state of stillness is practice.

In the second pada, we learn that concentration, leading to meditation, is binding the mind to a single point and in order to become proficient at this we must practice. Here in the first pada, we learn that stilling the citta and the vrtti also takes practice. We must learn to step away from the constant machinations of the mind to experience ourselves as the seers.

Meditation is the formal process of stilling the body and the mind while remaining alert, but we can do this as we move through our day fully engaged in our duties as well. It is a form of detachment Yogis learn to master. We understand life is not something we manipulate for our own purposes, but it is an expression of spirit we watch unfold, participating without egotistical involvement.

PADA I, SUTRA 14

Sa tu dirgha-kala-nairantarya-satkara-asevito drdha-bhumih

This but long-time-uninterrupted-properly-cultivated firmly-grounded

But this practice becomes firmly grounded when properly cultivated for a long time without interruption.

The practice of Yoga and meditation does not yield short term results for instant gratification; it requires steadfast dedication to the process for a prolonged period of time. For most of us, there is a gradual unfoldment of understanding, and realization comes as the outcome of a devoted practice. We become more efficient at stilling the mind, radically accepting current circumstances, coming to terms and resolving the past, and living in the present with grace and dignity.

As we learn to first recognize, then accept the kleshas which poison the mind, we begin to investigate their source in order to nullify their effects. Once resolved and neutralized, we are able to dissolve their mental impressions completely by righteous, conscious living and profound super-conscious meditation. This process necessitates patience, practice, and equanimity as we awaken to the truth of our existence-being.

Pada I, Sutra 15

Drsta-anusravika-visaya-vitrsnasya vasikara-samjna vairagyam

Seen-revealed-object-without thirst (desireless) mastery-knowledge dispassion

Mastery and knowledge, without desire, of any object or condition that has either been observed with the senses or revealed from within, is dispassion.

Here is the essence of Yogic radical acceptance; we train ourselves to see and understand any object or condition and accept it as it is without a desire for it to be anything other than what it is. We have no intent to change people, things, or circumstances for the sake of self-interest. We let go the need to manipulate life, presented to us in any form, in the forges of our imaginations or the machinations of our minds.

Self-realization requires absolute surrender to the intelligence Divine empowered within. We learn grace is not a potential external to us, but it is a presence within us; when we abide in this presence, no power external to it or contrary to it can stand. Fulfilled in this realization of truth, we are complete and whole without a desire for anything or any circumstance to be other than what it is.

Pada I, Sutra 16

Tat-param Purusa-khyater-guna-vaitrsnyam

That-highest Self-perception-quality of nature-without thirsting

With the realization of Self, all desire for experiences in the material realm ends.

Self-realization is wholly satisfying; the soul, once established in existence-being, no longer identifies with or is any longer curious about the material realm. There is an endless flowing of bliss intrinsic to soul-fulfillment that quenches any thirst for further involvement with nature. The soul, now knowing it is no longer the doer, responds only to the inspirations of spirit and is set free from the entanglements of future karma.

PADA I, SUTRA 17

Vitarka-vicara-ananda-asmita-anugamat-samprajnatah

Contemplation-reflection-bliss-I-am-ness(ego)- following-Samadhi with highest wisdom

The samadhi of highest wisdom (direct insight into truth) is accompanied by contemplation, reflection, bliss, and a separate sense of self.

When the citta and the vrtti have been purified and come to a complete standstill, the soul has the Self-directed experience of existence-being. It is through the lens of the buddhi that this transpires. Direct insight is a known-by-knowing experience. Though realization of Self occurs in this moment, there is still a sense of I-am-ness (ego), a separate sense of differentiated self which remains. There is still the seer… seeing. Awareness has not yet been so purified as to be completely transparent. There is a boundary designated by a subject and an object; I am that. This is not transcendent consciousness where there is no longer a boundary of awareness. It is superconsciousness with a pale difference between the seer and the seen.

PADA I, SUTRA 18

Virama-pratyaya-abhyasa-purvah samskara-seso'nyah

Cessation-intention-practice-former psycho-mental impression-residual other

Asamprajnatah only has a residual of mental impressions and is preceded by practice with the gentle intent to restrain completely the citta and the vrtti.

In the previous sutra, it is explained that samprajnatah, the samadhi of wisdom, while giving direct insight through realization, is accompanied with thoughts, impressions, bliss, and a separate sense of existence. In this sutra, we are told the highest level of samadhi, Asamprajnatah, no longer has gross thoughts, only the subtle residual of their impressions. But, more importantly, there is no longer the awareness of 'I am'. We become established in this consciousness by repeated experiences of samprajnatah samadhi.

This realization is said to occur by the grace of God, not as a result of any overt effort or action on our part. We rest in the awareness of oneness (one without a second) as spirit carries us the rest of the way home.

PADA I, SUTRA 19

Bhava-pratyayo videha-prakrti-layanam

Becoming-intention bodiless-primal nature-absorption in

Disembodied souls, still absorbed in and clinging to material creation, are intent on incarnating in this realm.

We leave this material realm when the physical body dies, but this does not mean our involvement with it or our desire to be involved with it ends. In order to dissolve our karma, we must resolve our karma. When we leave the body awakened to our spiritual truth, with all karma resolved, and without desire for further experiences, we are no longer compelled to return to this realm from the astral realm or beyond.

Souls who cling to having more experiences due to their desires, are obliged to reincarnate in this world until they have freed themselves from all karma by resolution, meditation, and realization.

PADA I, SUTRA 20

Sraddha-virya-smrti-samadhi-prajna-purvaka itaresam

Faith-energy-mindfulness-samadhi-wisdom-preceded by of the others

For those others who are not absorbed in, or clinging to prakriti (primal nature), yoga (union) is preceded by faith, energy, mindfulness, samadhi, and wisdom.

Detachment from the phenomenal world is a prerequisite to yoga. We cannot be absorbed in the delusional play of life going on around us and liberate ourselves from it. When, through practice, we learn to maintain our awareness as the observer, we become less emotionally and psychologically invested in appearances. With this acquired calmness and mindfulness comes a peace that is reinforced by our increased faith and our consciously directed energy. We begin to make choices which support our goal of God-Realization and uplift our awareness of our spiritual reality.

Final realization is preceded by increasing episodes of samadhi. With repeated experiences of Self-realization, we become established in spirit. This sutra seems to indicate that final union, yoga is reinforced by previous experiences of samadhi leading to the possible conclusion samadhi and yoga are not synonymous.

Pada I, Sutra 21

Tivra-samveganam asannah

Strong–intense ones near

The devotee whose practice is strongly intense is near the final goal.

Paramahansa Yogananda told my Guru, Roy Eugene Davis, to "Read a little, meditate more, think of God all the time." The more intently focused we are on a goal, the quicker we are likely to reach it. If we incorporate our spiritual practices into every aspect of our lives, while reminding ourselves to remain the observer, we will soon awaken. Meditation is only part of our spiritual practice; the other hours of the day are just as important. We can live consciously, dedicating our lives to the awakening process and committing to do what is necessary to become Self and God realized. If we live a moral life in harmony with our dharma and the laws of nature, yearning for liberation, we can only awaken that much sooner.

Pada I, Sutra 22

Mirdu-madhya-adhimatratvat-tato'pi visesah

Mild–moderate–ardent–hence also distinction

Hence, a distinction may also be made between those devotees whose practice is mild, moderate, or intense.

It should be self-evident our results on the spiritual path directly reflect our level of involvement and commitment. We are responsible for our own spiritual growth and evolution. There is no force outside ourselves that is in control of our successes or failures on the spiritual path. Our advancing stages of awakening are a reflection of our level of commitment. Our effort and focus will yield predictable outcomes. The more devoted and committed we are, the sooner we will experience success.

Pada I, Sutra 23

Isvara-pranidhanad va

Isvara (Lord)-devotion or

One is also near the goal who is devoted to the Lord.

The term pranidhana means 'to put before'. This is translated as devotion and this sutra is stating it is possible to awaken fully this lifetime through devotion or bhakti alone.

The root of the word bhakti is *bhaj*, which means 'to adore or worship'. It carries with it the connotation of devotional service. Devotion and service should be integrated into every aspect of our lives. By putting God foremost in our thoughts, as we move through the day serving humanity, we step unerringly towards the source.

Whether we ardently desire to know the Lord as a personified being or the ideal of awakening to the transcendental reality is our primary motivation, our unrelenting devotion will carry us forward to the goal.

To be devotional does not mean to be emotional; we can practice moment-to-moment equanimity while remaining devoted to God and the goal of God-realization. Quiet, less overtly emotional people, often have a profound and mystical relationship with God.

Pada I, Sutra 24

Klesa-karma-vipaka-asayair aparamrstah purusa-visesa isvarah

Affliction-action-fruition-residue (of karma) untouched Self-special Lord

Isvara is that special Self (Soul/Spirit), untouched by the five mental afflictions or the fruits and residue of karma.

This sutra defines Isvara as being that special, eternal and original spirit (purusa) from which all individual spirits (souls) are derived. It is unmodified and unaffected by the interaction of the citta, vrtti, kleshas or samskara. It remains the universal observer, untouched by the drama of creation.

The interaction of individualized spirit with primordial nature makes possible the expression of the multiverse while unmodified spirit remains aloof. It is possible that Patanjali's yoga sutras define Isvara here because they are breaking away from the tradition established in the Samkhya philosophy that a personified God is irrelevant. Here, the author seems to understand devotion to a personal God may be a vital step in one's spiritual evolution and should not be ignored.

Eventually, we will all leave behind a limited concept of God as we awaken to the omnipresent, omnipotent, and omniscient presence of spirit.

Pada I, Sutra 25

Tatra niratisayam sarva-jna-bijam

There unsurpassed all-knowing-seed

There the omniscient seed is unsurpassed.

The source of creation is unmodified universal existence-being, spirit. It is the eternal, enduring observer and omniscience is inherent to it. It is beyond the influence of the gunas and therefore considered to be spirit in its purest and unadulterated formless reality. There is nothing beyond it or more than it. It is the final boundless consciousness, surpassing all thought and form.

Pada I, Sutra 26

Purvesam-api guruh kalena-anavacchedat

Prior ones-also teacher time-boundless

Not bound by the limitations of time, Isvara (God) is also the teacher of those Yogis who came before.

All knowledge and realization of truth originates with the source. Spirit rests outside the bound framework of the time field and is therefore the one universal constant which has always been the teacher and inspiration of yogis. The mystic turns inward in silence and awaits the revelation that blossoms from the Divine within.

"I salute the supreme teacher, the truth, whose nature is bliss; Who is the giver of the highest happiness; who is pure wisdom; Who is beyond all qualities and infinite like the sky; Who is one and eternal, pure and still; Who is beyond all change and phenomena and the silent to our thoughts and emotions. I salute truth, the supreme teacher." -----Ancient Vedic Hymn

PADA I, SUTRA 27

Tasya vacakah pranavag

Its expression pronouncement (sacred syllable) (OM)

The sacred syllable of OM is the outward expression of Isvara (God).

OM is referred to by mystics as the vibrational hum that emanates from the source. It is the bija (seed) mantra of all other mantras and is a morpheme; this sound and syllable cannot be further divided into sub sounds or syllables and is therefore considered to be the fundamental progenitor of all other sounds and mantras.

In the Kriya Yoga tradition, we contemplate OM by listening to the inner sounds, becoming absorbed in them and allowing them to lead us ever inward to the source. If OM emanates from the source, we can use it to return to the source.

PADA I, SUTRA 28

Taj Japas tad artha-bhavanam

That repetition that meaning realization

Recitation of OM and contemplation of its meaning leads to realization.

Using OM as a mantra will assist in the interiorization process, eventually allowing us to transcend the mind and its limitations. Repeating OM verbally, then mentally, and finally listening to the inner sounds gives us an object on which to concentrate.

Meditation begins when concentration flows uninterrupted, leading our awareness to the source of the sound. It is possible to then experience samadhi from the practice of this mantra meditation alone. Meditation on OM invites more subtle experiences and more profound realizations.

PADA I, SUTRA 29

Tatah pratyakcetana-adhigamo'py-antaraya-abhavas-ca

Thence inward mindedness-attainment also-obstacle-disappearance

As a consequence of meditating on OM, one experiences interiorization and the removal of obstacles.

The mind is easily interiorized and quieted with the repetition and contemplation of *OM*. The citta and the vrtti effortlessly begin to still and the process becomes dynamic. The meditator finds a singular clarity and focus that is difficult to attain using other meditation methods. The usual obstacles to meditation such as poor concentration and a busy mind are overcome as the sound of *OM* resonates through the mental field. Meditation and the contemplation of *OM* also assist the devotee in overcoming the many other obstacles listed in the next sutra by rerouting neural pathways, improving memory, and cauterizing poor habits and inclinations.

OM captures the attention and assists in the process of concentration on a single point, object, or concept. With this one-pointed focus, the meditator more easily transcends the movement and restrictions of the mind.

Pada I, Sutra 30

Vyadhi-styana-samsaya-pramada-alasya-avirati-bhranti-darsana-alabdha-bhumikatva-anavasthitatvani-citta-viksepas-te'ntarayah

Sickness-dullness-doubt-carelessness-sloth-sense indulgence-false views-nonattainment-stage-instability-consciousness-distraction-these obstacles

The distracting obstacles to Yoga (union) are: sickness, dullness, doubt, carelessness, indolence, wrong use of vital energies, false beliefs, not attaining successive stages of realization, inconsistent practice, and lack of awareness.

Yogis must be ever vigilante in their pursuit of the Divine. The mind is easily distracted and the enticements of the world can seem irresistible. Our devotion to God and the goal of liberation requires a continual, lifelong commitment.

We learn to responsibly and joyfully interact with life, keeping our eyes on God, while we navigate the world cultivating our inner peace. We practice being the observer behind the mind, watching as life unfolds before us. Inwardly, we keep our thoughts upon the Divinity within while outwardly living a righteous and moral life. We become relentless spiritual warriors ever marching towards the goal.

PADA I, SUTRA 31

Duhkha-daurmanasya-angam-ejayatva-svasa-prasvasa viksepa-sahabhuvah

Suffering–depression–limb–unsteadiness–inhalation–exhalation–distraction–accompanying

Accompanying the distractions are suffering, depression, unsteadiness of body, and unsteadiness of breath.

As we transform the citta, vrtti, kleshas, and samskara (our karmic package), into pure conduits through which spirit flows, there are often both psychological and physical challenges to face. It may become necessary to seek out qualified counselors to assist us in this process. There is a reason it is referred to as inner work.

Self-actualization often coincides with Self-realization. Radical acceptance, surrender, and coming to terms with the past are all part of the transformative yoga process. Some karma we must experience, some karma can be overcome, and some karma can be transcended, but all karma must be faced. Equipping ourselves with vital emotional tools to successfully navigate the inner psychological terrain will further support and enhance our spiritual evolution.

PADA I, SUTRA 32

Tat pratisedha-artham-eka-tattva-abhyasah

That counteracting–purpose single–(that-ness)–practice

To counteract the distractions and obstacles, practice a single principle listed in the next sutra.

When we overly focus on ourselves and our own problems, we may become self-absorbed and obsessive. To counteract the tendency to play the role of victim and be small minded and egotistical, we can adopt a more altruistic attitude and help others on their spiritual journeys.

When we place others first regardless of how we feel, it strengthens our mental capacity, reinforces a positive attitude, and it takes our mind off our superficial self-interests. This new selfless viewpoint breaks down mental barriers, creating greater space for expansion of consciousness.

When we think and behave in self-sacrificing ways, we learn to let go of that small, separate sense of I-am-ness and allow ourselves the opportunity to have a more universal experience of spiritual unity.

Pada I, Sutra 33

Maitri-karuna-mudita-upeksanam sukha-duhkha-punya-apunya-visayanam bhavanatas citta prasadanam

Friendliness-compassion-gladness-equanimity-joyfullness-suffering-meritorious-demertorious-conditions from cultivation consciousness pacification

Clarify the consciousness and pacify the mind under both auspicious and inauspicious conditions by cultivating friendliness, compassion, gladness, equanimity, and joyfulness.

To behave righteously with calm dignity, regardless of the circumstances we are under, clarifies and strengthens the mind making us fit conduits for spirit. We can train ourselves to remain inwardly peaceful no matter what is occurring in the world around us.

Collectively, friendliness, compassion, gladness, and equanimity are referred to as the 'stations of Brahma'. Here, the sutras suggest consciously practicing one of them at a time. This not only cleanses the mind; it also helps prepare the mind for more profound meditation experiences which require refined levels of concentration and focus.

Better still is to practice remaining the observer while interacting with the world from friendliness, compassion, gladness, equanimity, and joyfulness.

Pada I, Sutra 34

Pracchardana-Vidharanabhyam va pranasya

Expulsion-retention or (breath/lifeforce)

Pranayama may be used to counteract suffering, depression, unsteadiness of body, and unsteadiness of breath.

By consciously practicing pranayama, we can calm and balance the mind, focus our thoughts, strengthen and make steady the body, assisting in the mature resolution of difficult circumstances.

Pranayama is a powerful and effective tool in the spiritual process when yoga and meditation dredge up subconscious drives, habits, tendencies, and patterns to be cleared out, resolved, and dissolved by the conscious mind.

The breath and the mind are intimately connected. By calming and balancing the breath, we calm and balance the mind. To deliberately place the mind on the breath changes its focus from the negative and places the attention elsewhere. The simple act of intentional breathing anchors us in the present, eliminating the fear that accompanies the ego when confronted with the need to release attachment, aversion, and clinging.

PADA I, SUTRA 35

Visaya-vati va pravrttir-utpanna manasah sthiti-nibandani

Object-centered or activity arisen mind steadiness-binding

Steadiness of the mind can come from binding the mind to an object centered activity.
When we place the mind on an object centered activity, we stabilize it through concentration and focus. When we concentrate on an activity which requires attention to detail, the mind brings to bear all its resources to accomplish the task. The mind and breath quiet, balancing and encouraging prana to flow smoothly as well. This leaves no energy available for worry or obsession.

We temporarily let go of what is troubling us in order to accomplish the task placed before us; by focusing on a single object, principle, or ideal, we allow the conscious mind to refresh itself while the subconscious works out the challenge without interference. Often when we temporarily take our minds off our problems, we find when we return to them, they have been resolved.

PADA I, SUTRA 36

Visoka va Jyotismati

Sorrowless or having illumination

Steadiness of the mind can come from experiencing sorrowless illumination.
With repeated experiences of samadhi, Neural pathways are rerouted, destructive patterns are cauterized, reasoning and motor skills are improved, and higher cognitive levels are experienced.

As we awaken to the reality of our existence, we see clearer and are less influenced by external circumstances. We understand change is built into the fabric of our existence, and with this understanding comes the ability to adapt and overcome.

In meditation we experience increasing degrees of inner peace and over time, with practice, we learn to maintain this inner peace throughout our waking lives as we interact with our world.

Pada I, Sutra 37

Vita-raga-visayam va cittam

Free from–attachment or consciousness

Steadiness of the mind can come from the consciousness being free from attachment.
All expressions of spirit bound by nature are subject to change. There is an ebb and flow to life, and change is the tide which begins and ends all things. Everyone and everything have their moment of expression, and to be attached to that expression is to experience loss and grief when its time comes to an end.

One of the greatest spiritual lessons and challenge is to love without attachment and without expectation. Hold life too tightly and it will break in your grasp, too loosely and it will slip away. To interact with life knowing it is the way of all things to rise up, express, then fall away, is to appreciate what you have without clinging to it.

To understand the temporal nature of this world brings with it a surrender and an acceptance to life. The mind finds peace and a clarity of purpose with this understanding.

Pada I, Sutra 38

Svapna-nidra-jn ana-alambanam va

Dream-sleep-knowledge-resting on or

Steadiness of the mind can come from resting on the knowledge gained from sleep and dreams.
The more awake we become, the more we gain the ability to consciously dream. This gives us one more tool to clarify the mind and its contents. Dreams are the symbolic language of the mind and often assist us in bringing the

subconscious to the surface, allowing us to resolve attachments, aversions, and clinging, in order to dissolve them.

When we become conscious participants in our dreams, we can be more aware of what we need to look at and let go. Dreaming is less about the actual dream and more about the unresolved feelings we have that accompany the dream. When we awake, it is the feelings we need to resolve, not the dream itself.

Pada I, Sutra 39

Yatha-abhimata-dhyanad-va

As-desired-meditation-or

Steadiness of the mind can come from meditation as desired.

Many studies have clearly shown a connection between meditation and brain health. Meditation increases neuroplasticity, relieves anxiety, pain, and depression. Long time meditators have been shown to have thicker frontal lobes, the part of the brain responsible for reasoning, motor skills, higher level cognition, and expressive language.

Profound meditation balances the left and right hemispheres of the brain, calming emotions, and promoting clear thinking.

Pada I, Sutra 40

Parama-anu-parama-mahattva-anto'sya vasikarah

Most-minute-greatest-greatness-(from…to)-his mastery

A yogi's mastery of the mind ranges from the smallest to the greatest.

The practice of yoga, concentration, and meditation encourages mastery over the functions of the brain. We learn to remain the observer under all circumstances regardless of their perceived influence, and in doing so, we become more aware and conscious of our decision-making abilities.

We empower ourselves to choose life enhancing thoughts, words, and actions as a result of our spiritual practices and disciplines. We can choose to interact as a conscious observer participating in the drama we call life. The more awake and aware we are, the more choice we have to be masters over our internal environment.

Pada I, Sutra 41

Ksina-vrtter-abhijatasya-iva
maner-grahitr-grahana-grahyesu-tat-stha-tad-anjananata-samapattih

Diminished-fluctuations-precious-like jewel-
grasper-grasping-grasped that-standing-that-made clear-unity

The mind, diminished of fluctuations and made clear, like a precious jewel, assumes unity with the grasper, grasping, and grasped.

When the mind is purified and the whirling movements of the vrtti are stilled, it becomes a refined and clear conduit through which spirit may fully express in the world. Once clarified, the Buddhi becomes a radiant mirror in which the self is reflected. The soul then abides in its own form and likeness in unity with spirit.

The seer sees that which is to be seen without bias, error, and fantasy. The true essence of spirit is then realized. This state of realization is a rare and precious thing in nature and uplifts humanity.

Pada I, Sutra 42

Tatra sabda-artha-jnana-viklpaih samkirna savitarka samapattih

In that word-meaning-knowledge-imagination interspersed with thought unity

Concept, imagination, and understanding are comingled while experiencing Savikalpa Samadhi.

In Savikalpa Samadhi, an echo of I-am-ness is still retained. Though a sense of unity has been achieved, the meditator perceives him or herself as 'I am one with the object of my meditation now'. We experience such thoughts as 'I am light' or 'I am sound'. We can still name the experience. The mind continues to function because it has not been completely transcended.

Sometimes subtle or gross thoughts continue to pass across the tableau of our consciousness at this level of attainment. It is at this stage of spiritual development we must be particularly careful not to be caught up in fantasy. Always while meditating have the gentle intention to go further, asking "Is there more?"

Pada I, Sutra 43

Smriti-parisuddhau sva rupa-sunya-iva-artha-matra-nirbhasa nirvitarka

*Memory-purified own form-empty-as it
were-meaning-only-shines forth beyond thought*

*Samadhi occurs when the memory is purified. Then, the mind becomes transparent
and is transcended with only its purpose remaining.*

When the mind has been purged of its remaining past memories, the last of
its karma has been purified making it a fit vessel through which spirit may fully
express. Spirit then shines without obstruction; the soul is completely awake.

The illumined soul is no longer identified with the contents of the mind and
is able to intentionally use the mind for the sole purpose it was intended. We are
here to awaken and once we are awake, it is then our responsibility to assist others
in the awakening process.

Pada I, Sutra 44

Etayaiva savicara nirvicara ca suksma-visaya vyakhyata

By this-thus savicara samadhi nirvicara samadhi and subtle condition explained

Thus, this also explains the subtle conditions of savicara samadhi and nirvicara samadhi.

Within Patanjali's Yoga there are as many as ten different types of samadhi
delineated. Savicara and nirvicara are considered to preliminary samadhis with
an element of thought and effort still involved.

This sutra reinforces that purification of the citta and vrtti and the resultant
samadhi are attained as a consequence of meditation, proper thought, behavior,
and personal effort. With practice and patience, we can achieve the steadiness of
mind required to experience Self-realization.

Pada I, Sutra 45

Suksma-visayatvam ca alinga-paryavasanam

Subtle-condition and undesignated terminate

And the subtle condition ends in the unmanifest field of absolute existence-being.

By repeated experiences of samadhi, we become established in Self-realization As we continue to dissolve the boundaries of ego and the veil of maya falls away we eventually become established in pure existence-being, God-realization. No longer identified with an individualized perception or personified understanding and experience of God, the soul is referred to as jivan mukti, 'free while embodied'

The final stage of liberation is the dissolution of any separate sense of existence At this stage of spiritual awakening, absolute surrender is required as we merge into the wholeness of spirit.

Pada I, Sutra 46

Ta eva sabijah samadhih

These indeed with seed samadhi

The previously described samadhis are with seed.

During early stages of samadhi, a separate sense of an individualized existence lingers. There is still the viewpoint of the observer having the experience: "I am light, I am bliss, I am OM..." The subject and object remain and the ego persists, therefore the seed of delusion persists.

With repeated experiences, boundaries between the individual soul and universal spirit break down and the seed idea of a separate existence dissolves, leading to absolute unity; one without a second, is established. This is referred to a nirbija, or samadhi without seed. With this realization, the curtain of maya drops away leaving only the experience of existence-being.

Pada I, Sutra 47

Nirvicara-vaisaradye dhyatma-prasadah

Beyond reflection-skill in soul clarity

The skill and mastery of Samadhi beyond thought establishes one in soul clarity.

Repeated experiences of Samadhi result in permanent God–realization. When the Soul becomes unwaveringly anchored in the realization of its unity with Spirit, there is no longer a false sense of separate reality; there is the perfect harmony that can only be found in the reality of existence-being. This is accomplished through practice, patience, and perseverance.

The goal of liberation and the end to suffering requires honest self-analysis, emotional maturity, commitment, righteous living, and profound states of meditative super-consciousness.

PADA I, SUTRA 48

Rtam-bhara tatra prajna

Truth-bearing in that wisdom

The insight of this wisdom is truth bearing.
Established in existence-being, we clearly perceive the truth and its wisdom guides our thoughts, words, and deeds. God is the creation, flow, and dissolution of the manifest realms. When we awaken to the realization of this truth, we are free from delusion and the mistaken belief we are separate from the source.

In this realization of truth, there is wisdom and the banishment of ignorance endures. We then walk the world in perfect accord with the will of God. We are guided by the unerring Divine intelligence that is available to us all.

PADA I, SUTRA 49

Sruta-anumana-prajnabhyam-anya-visaya-visesa-arthatvat

Tradition-inference-wisdom-different-condition-distinct-purpose

The wisdom of this samadhi is different from the wisdom gained by tradition and inference because of its distinct purpose.
The wisdom gained by the experience of this *Samadhi of wisdom* is beyond that of conventional knowledge. It is the wisdom born from the realization of truth. It is free of a bias perspective or opinion. It is direct insight into the core of an object, concept, or idea.

The mind must take in and process information which can be correct, in error, or partially correct, partially incorrect. But the soul has the ability to simply know-by-knowing through realization. There is no intermediary between the seer and that which is seen. The insight is pure, without the taint of perspective or opinion; it is direct and complete insight through intuition.

Pada I, Sutra 50

Taj-jah samskaro nya-samskara-pratibandhi

That-born psycho-mental impression-other-psycho-mental impression-obstructs

The samskara that come from the experience of Samadhi, obstructs the samskara from other experiences.

The experience of Samadhi invites superconscious forces to flood the mind, cauterizing negative mental impressions left there by previous experiences. These forces purify, reorganize, and refine the brain and mind making them fit conduits through which spirit may flow unobstructed and untainted.

Over time, repeated experiences of Samadhi continue to refine the mind and its organ, the brain. The meditator becomes calmer, clearer, and less attached to outcomes. Eventually, the soul is fully awake and consciously uses the mind as the tool of interaction it was meant to be.

Pada I, Sutra 51

Tasya api nirodha sarva-nirodhan nirbija samadhih

Of this even restricted all-restricted seedless samadhi

With even this restricted, all is restricted and that is seedless samadhi.

Lastly, when even the samskara of samadhi are restricted, purified, and removed, there is complete stillness within the individual field of consciousness and the soul rests in the absoluteness of existence-being. It is then that the second sutra is fully realized: 'Yoga Citta Vrtti Nirodha'.

Conclusion

What lies behind you and what lies in front of you,
pales in comparison to what lies within you.
— Ralph Waldo Emerson

When all the moving parts within the field of our awareness have ground to a halt, when the stillness of pure existence-being is the only awareness we have, and when the barriers of the mind that prevent the soul from realizing its true identity have been dissolved, union through Yoga is achieved. The faithful practice of Yoga undeterrably transforms the individual consciousness from awareness as a limited and self-centered ego to the realization of boundless and universal spirit.

The art and science of Yoga provides those seeking liberation from suffering and those seeking the truth, the practical steps needed to be free. Yoga is the mystical solution to suffering made an empirical and practical reality. It provides for those truth seekers looking to awaken to their spiritual Divinity, a proven means to do so.

Yoga renders religious doctrine and philosophy superfluous by offering useful spiritual sensibilities; it delivers clear and concise instructions that when adhered to, lead to the goal of Self- and God-realization.

The Nirodha Yoga of Patanjali's Yoga Sutras elucidates the challenges facing every spiritual aspirant and guides the devotee of God through the process of overcoming them. By faithfully practicing Yoga, the spiritual disciple removes all barriers between the Soul and Spirit. With patience, practice, and perseverance, the soul returns itself to wholeness through Yoga; our practice becomes an integrated way of life. Yoga is an all-encompassing journey to liberation and spiritual fulfillment which requires our dedicated commitment.

Once free, the soul will never again submit to the shackles of unknowing. The bliss of existence-being and the realization of God within, is a rare and priceless spiritual achievement that must be earned by the steadfast practice of Yoga. We must never give up and never concede defeat; we can find God this lifetime and return to the joy of wholeness, experienced by the realization of God through Yoga.

About the Author

Michael Gadway began his spiritual studies with Roy Eugene Davis in 1988 and was ordained by him into the Kriya Yoga tradition in 2003. He has made a profound examination of the Vedic sciences including Ayurveda and Vedic Astrology with Dr. David Frawley, and an intense study of Patanjali's Yoga Sutras, The Bhagavad Gita, Samkhya Philosophy, and The Upanishads under the guidance of Roy Eugene Davis.

Michael received a BA in English from St. Lawrence University later becoming a Chiropractic physician with a degree from the University of Western States.

He teaches truth principles and the liberating science of Kriya Yoga and Yoga Psychology. His books include, *The Yoga of Healing*, *The Ashtanga Yoga of Patanjali: The eightfold Path to Liberation*, *The Kriya Yoga of Patanjali: The Art and Science of Self Realization*, *The Nirodha Yoga of Patanjali: The Transformation of Consciousness*, and *The Yoga Sutras Workbook*.

References

Aranya, H. Yoga Philosophy of Patanjali. Albany,
    NY: State University of New York Press, 1963.

Chapple, Christopher, and Yogi Anand Viraj.
    The Yoga Sūtras of Patañjali: An Analysis of the Sanskrit with Accompanying English Translation.
    Delhi: Sri Satguru Publications, 1990.

Davis, Roy Eugene. *This Is Reality*.
    Lakemont, GA: CSA Press, 1962.

Davis, Roy Eugene. *The Science of Kriya Yoga*.
    Lakemont, GA: CSA Press, 1984.

Davis, Roy Eugene. *An Easy Guide to Meditation*.
    Lakemont, GA: CSA Press, 1988.

Davis, Roy Eugene. *Life Surrendered in God: The Kriya Yoga Way of Soul Liberation*.
    Lakemont, GA: CSA Press, 1995.

Davis, Roy Eugene. *The Science of Self-realization*.
    Lakemont, GA: CSA Press, 2004.

Eliade, Mircea. *Yoga: Immortality and Freedom*.
    Princeton, NJ: Princeton University Press, 1958.

Feuerstein, Georg. *The Yoga-sutra of Patanjali: A New Translation and Commentary*.
    Rochester, VT: Inner Traditions International, 1979.

Houston, Vyaas. *The Yoga Sutra Workbook: The Certainty of Freedom.*
Collingswood, NJ: American Sanskrit Institute, 1995.

Klostermaier, Klaus K. *Hindu Writings: A Short Introduction to the Major Sources.*
Boston, MA: Oneworld Publications, 2000.

Monier-Williams, M. *A Sanskrit-English Dictionary.*
New Delhi, India: Bharatiya Granth Niketan, 2015.

Vivekananda, S. *Raja Yoga.*

White, David Gordon. *The Yoga Sutra of Patanjali: A Biography.*
Princeton, NJ: Princeton University Press, 2014.

Woods, James Haughton. *The Yoga-System of Patanjali.*
Cambridge, MA: Harvard University Press, 1914.

Yogananda, Paramahansa. *God Talks with Ajuna: The Bhagavad Gita.*
Los Angeles, CA: Internal Publications Council of
Self-Realization Fellowship, 1995.